Stepping Into

MARK TWAIN'S WORLD

Torrey Maloof

Consultants

Timothy Rasinski, Ph.D.
Kent State University

Lori Oczkus, M.A.
Literacy Consultant

Publishing Credits

Rachelle Cracchiolo, M.S.Ed., *Publisher*
Conni Medina, M.A.Ed., *Managing Editor*
Dona Herweck Rice, *Series Developer*
Emily R. Smith, M.A.Ed., *Content Director*
Stephanie Bernard/Susan Daddis, M.A.Ed., *Editors*
Robin Erickson, *Senior Graphic Designer*

The TIME logo is a registered trademark of TIME Inc. Used under license.

Image Credits: Cover and p.1 LOC [LC-USZC4-9893]; p.5 Mary Evans Picture Library/Alamy Stock Photo; p.6 NASA/NSSDC; p.8 Wikimedia Commons/Public Domain; pp.10–11 TTstudio/Shutterstock.com; pp.12–13 f11photo/Shutterstock.com; p.14 Internet Archive/Public Domain; pp.14–15, 18, 19, 22–23, 24–25, 26, 34–35 North Wind Picture Archives; p.16 Mariners Museum; p.17 LOC [LC-USZ62-77201]; pp.20–21 Universal History Archive/UIG via Getty Images; p.33 Granger, NYC; p.39 Mary Evans Picture Library/Alamy Stock Photo; p.40 (left) SSPL/Getty Images, (top) Timothy Malone/EyeEm/Getty Image; pp.42–43 GL Archive/Alamy Stock Photo; all other images from iStock and/or Shutterstock.

Library of Congress Cataloging-in-Publication Data

Names: Maloof, Torrey, author.
Title: The world of Mark Twain / Torrey Maloof.
Description: Huntington Beach, CA : Teacher Created Materials, 2017. | Includes index.
Identifiers: LCCN 2016026810 (print) | LCCN 2016044593 (ebook) | ISBN 9781493836208 (pbk.) | ISBN 9781480757240 (eBook)
Subjects: LCSH: Twain, Mark, 1835-1910--Juvenile literature. | Authors, American--19th century--Biography--Juvenile literature. | Humorists, American--19th century--Biography--Juvenile literature.
Classification: LCC PS1331 .M18 2017 (print) | LCC PS1331 (ebook) | DDC 818/.409 [B] --dc23
LC record available at https://lccn.loc.gov/2016026810

Teacher Created Materials

5301 Oceanus Drive
Huntington Beach, CA 92649-1030
http://www.tcmpub.com

ISBN 978-1-4938-3620-8
© 2017 Teacher Created Materials, Inc.

Table of Contents

n older-looking man sits relaxed in a chair, wearing
mmer suit of soft, light cotton. The suit, like his
what unruly hair, is all white. He has bushy
ows and a thick but classic mustache—all of which
ite. He holds a serious and steady gaze. Who is
an? He is Mark Twain, one of America's favorite
ost famous writers.

hard to imagine the man in white as a redheaded,
aired boy running barefoot and wild. In the
the young Twain caused mischief and mayhem on
ks of the Mississippi River. Much like his beloved
ers Huckleberry Finn and Tom Sawyer, Twain's
od was spent in a river city in Missouri. While
n was had, Twain also witnessed slavery, racism,
ent crimes. His nineteenth century American
ing shaped his literary career, while his wit,
nd imagination made Mark Twain a household
y stepping into his world, we can see how his
dings and experiences influenced Twain's tales of
adventure.

The Truth Behind the Suit

Twain's trademark white suit made him
stand out in a crowd. But the truth is
that Mark Twain did not start wearing
this signature style until he was in his
seventies. He only wore the all-white
suits occasionally, but today many people
remember Twain as "the man in white."

Cigars and Cats

Two of Twain's favorite things were cigars and cats. He smoked more than 22 cigars a day. And it was not uncommon to see him carrying a cat around on his shoulders. He loved cats and would often tell his children bedtime stories about his furry feline friends.

The Great Storyteller

Halley's **Comet** appears about every 76 years. The bright streak of gas and dust was visible in the night sky the day Samuel Langhorne Clemens was born. That is Twain's real name. He came into the world two months early, on November 30, 1835, in the tiny town of Florida, Missouri. Twain's mother was worried that her **premature** baby wouldn't survive. Perhaps the comet brought him luck because Twain not only survived but lived a long, eventful life.

Twain Trivia

There is an attraction at Disneyland in Anaheim, California, called the Mark Twain Riverboat. If you ride the boat, you can hear a recording say, "Mark twain!" as you pull away from the dock. The island the river surrounds was originally called Tom Sawyer's Island and was based on Twain's book.

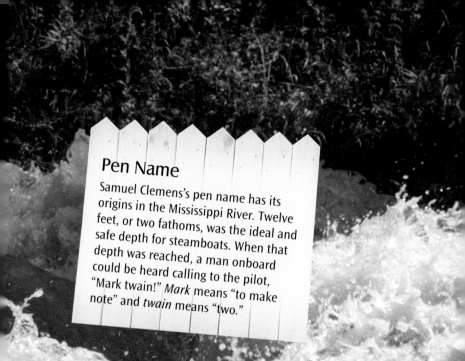

Pen Name

Samuel Clemens's pen name has its origins in the Mississippi River. Twelve feet, or two fathoms, was the ideal and safe depth for steamboats. When that depth was reached, a man onboard could be heard calling to the pilot, "Mark twain!" *Mark* means "to make note" and *twain* means "two."

Younger Years

Twain was a spirited, rambunctious young boy. He moved with his family to Hannibal, Missouri, in 1839. Twain described Hannibal as a "boy's paradise" with caves, islands, and woods for exploring. As a young boy, he would regularly skip school to play and go on adventures with his friends. Sometimes, they would fish or swim in the Mississippi River. Twain recalls almost drowning in the rough river on multiple occasions. One of Twain's favorite things to do was watch steamboats work their way down the watery path. The three-story powerful boats with their mighty smokestacks and giant paddlewheels called to Twain. He knew that one day he would pilot one of those majestic vessels.

A Printer's Apprentice

In 1847, Twain's father died, leaving the family financially strained. Twain quit school and became a printer's apprentice. He didn't earn money as an apprentice. Payment came in the form of learning new skills. However, Twain used these skills to get a job working for his older brother, Orion, who owned a local newspaper. But by the age of 17, Twain was tired of life in Hannibal and wanted to experience new adventures. He began to travel from city to city, picking up printing jobs where he could. He visited St. Louis, New York, and Chicago, among other places.

The six-cylinder printing press, patented in 1847, sped up the printing process.

A Nation Divided

From 1861 to 1865, the United States fought the violent and bloody Civil War. The issue at the core of the war was slavery, which the South relied on to keep its large **plantations** running. The decision of 11 southern states to **secede** from the **Union** and form the Confederacy prompted a civil war between the North and the South. The North won the war, slavery was abolished, and the Union was preserved.

Piloting the Mississippi

In 1857, Twain grew weary and restless again. He wanted new challenges and new adventures. He thought about the steamboats he loved as a child and decided to get a pilot's certificate. Horace Bixby, a celebrated steamboat pilot, let Twain be his apprentice. Twain had to learn how the boats worked as well as all the ins and outs of the long and winding Mississippi River. In 1859, Twain received his certificate. He worked as a pilot on the river until the Civil War broke out in 1861, which brought a stop to all commercial river traffic.

Westward Ho!

Shortly after the Civil War began, Twain traveled west to the Nevada Territory in search of silver. After he lost his savings fruitlessly looking for the precious metal, he began to write short news stories to make money. A newspaper in Virginia City, Nevada, hired him. He soon became known as one of the wittiest writers in the West. His writing was different from other articles. His work was amusing, mischievous, and sometimes **outlandish**. Readers loved Twain's biting humor. In 1864, Twain moved to San Francisco, California. Around that time, his writings were becoming more and more popular across the country.

A Petrified Man

In one of his early newspaper stories, Twain wrote about a man who had died centuries ago and turned to stone. While the story was a hoax, many newspapers printed the story as if it were true.

Virginia City, Nevada

Witty Worldly Writer

In 1867, Twain was again in search of more adventure. He embarked on a cruise to Europe and the Middle East. Newspapers paid Twain to send in humor-filled letters about his travels. The always **impish** Twain wrote funny observations about some of the world's most cherished locations and artifacts. For example, he said Leonardo da Vinci's *The Last Supper* was a "mournful wreck." His letters were so well received by American audiences that a publisher asked Twain to turn them into a book. He did, and *The Innocents Abroad* became a bestseller.

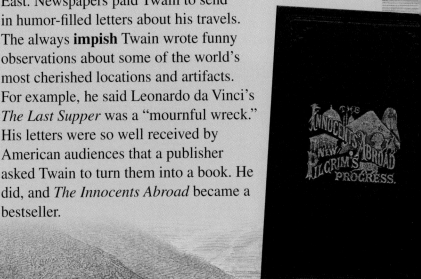

A Jumping Frog

A story that brought Twain fame in his early days was "The Celebrated Jumping Frog of Calaveras County." While the story is brief and simple, it is the way that Twain tells it that makes it so memorable.

Twain's Catalog

Although he is best known for creating Tom Sawyer and Huckleberry Finn, Twain penned 28 books and many short stories. He wrote about a man transported back in time to medieval England in *A Connecticut Yankee in King Arthur's Court*. Twain's time spent in the Wild West is captured in his book called *Roughing It*. He also wrote an autobiography.

Mark Twain's house in Hartford, Connecticut

Twain's Masterpiece

Twain, now 35 years old, was a famous and popular author. After his trip abroad, he met and married Livy Langdon. The couple built a home in Hartford, Connecticut, and had four children, a son and three daughters. Sadly, their son, Langdon, passed away before the age of two.

In the summer of 1874, Twain began work on *The Adventures of Tom Sawyer*. The book that introduced Tom and Huckleberry to the world would soon become one of the most popular stories in American history. Just like Twain's life, the story is packed full of adventure and witty characters. In 1884, Twain's masterpiece, *The Adventures of Huckleberry Finn*, was published. It, too, is full of adventure as Huck makes his way down the Mississippi River with a runaway slave named Jim. Despite harsh reviews upon its publication, the book later became an American classic.

When reading Twain's books, it is easy to see how his world influenced his stories. The more we know about this time period, the better we are able to understand and appreciate his work.

Controversial Content

Early critics condemned *The Adventures of Huckleberry Finn* for its use of coarse and rough language. Huck, as the narrator, does not use proper grammar or speak in an elevated and educated way. This offended many people in Twain's day. The book has remained controversial throughout its history, in large part due to its use of racial **epithets**.

The Mighty Mississippi

Today, networks of highways, railroads, and bustling airports transport goods and people. In Twain's world, the transportation of goods and people was managed on the mighty Mississippi River. The river not only played a central role in Twain's literary works and life but also in the history of America.

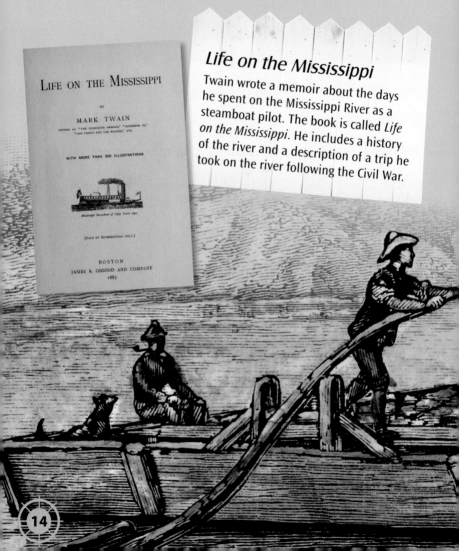

LIFE ON THE MISSISSIPPI

BY

MARK TWAIN

AUTHOR OF "THE INNOCENTS ABROAD," "ROUGHING IT,"
"THE PRINCE AND THE PAUPER," ETC.

WITH MORE THAN 300 ILLUSTRATIONS

Mississippi Steamboat of Fifty Years Ago.

[SOLD BY SUBSCRIPTION ONLY.]

BOSTON
JAMES R. OSGOOD AND COMPANY
1883

Life on the Mississippi

Twain wrote a memoir about the days he spent on the Mississippi River as a steamboat pilot. The book is called *Life on the Mississippi*. He includes a history of the river and a description of a trip he took on the river following the Civil War.

America was changing in the 1800s. Previously, the ocean had been used to move goods and people around the East Coast. But now, people were moving west! With westward expansion came a need to transport people and things to the middle of the country. Thanks to the Mississippi River, moving items south was easy enough; people used large flatboats, barges, and **keelboats**. However, moving cargo north, back up the river, was another story. The current was strong. Sometimes, people used long poles to push the boats upstream, but this was difficult, costly, and slow going. In 1805, everything changed with the invention of the steamboat!

Steamboats made transportation down and *up* the river quick, easy, and cost effective. By 1830, there were more than 200 steamboats traveling on the river. Thirty years later, there were more than 1,000! These were the river's golden years. The steamboats brought people from all walks of life right through Twain's world.

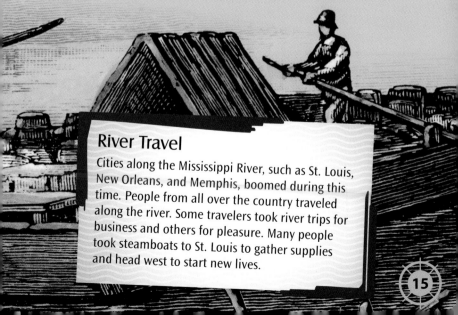

River Travel

Cities along the Mississippi River, such as St. Louis, New Orleans, and Memphis, boomed during this time. People from all over the country traveled along the river. Some travelers took river trips for business and others for pleasure. Many people took steamboats to St. Louis to gather supplies and head west to start new lives.

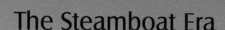

The Steamboat Era

From 1805 to 1861, steamboats ruled the Mississippi River. Here are some interesting facts about the golden era of the steamboat.

Pilot's Certificate

Being a steamboat pilot required learning a lot of new things:

- strength of currents in the river
- terms for measuring water depths
- shorelines and the shapes of rivers
- landmarks along the rivers
- how weather affects rivers
- parts of the boat and how they work

Pilot Perks

Steamboat pilots had many **perks** that came with the job:

- high salaries
- elegant uniforms
- fancy meals

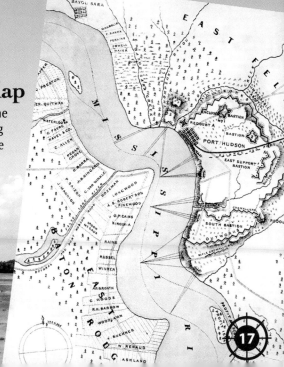

Danger!

Steamboats were not entirely safe and had many problems:

- boiler explosions
- fires
- hitting sunken steamboats
- running into sandbars or rocks
- collisions with other steamboats

Mississippi Map

This map shows some of the twists and turns of the long interstate river. You can see why it was tough to be a steamboat pilot!

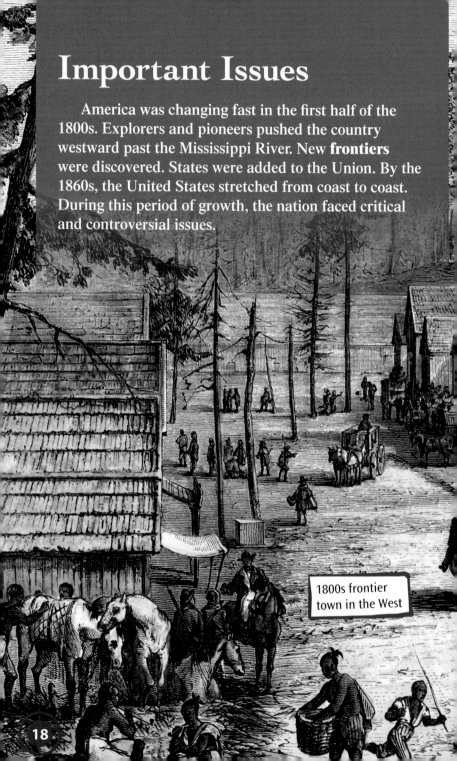

Important Issues

America was changing fast in the first half of the 1800s. Explorers and pioneers pushed the country westward past the Mississippi River. New **frontiers** were discovered. States were added to the Union. By the 1860s, the United States stretched from coast to coast. During this period of growth, the nation faced critical and controversial issues.

1800s frontier town in the West

Greed and Racism

Twain's world was one of change and conflict. The hunger for wealth drove many **migrants** west in search of gold and silver. Manifest Destiny was the belief that America had the ordained right to control the continent from "sea to shining sea." There was a belief that any man, no matter his social status, could become rich. But this belief did not apply to everyone.

Racism was common and widespread. Most white people thought their race was superior to other races. At that time, some white people saw American Indians as savages and viewed African Americans as property. Both groups faced prejudice and violence at every turn because of their skin color. They were not seen as equals, and they were denied the same rights and privileges that white citizens freely enjoyed.

Gold Rush

When word spread that gold had been discovered in California, migrants flocked to the West Coast with hopes of striking it rich. But mining was dangerous and difficult work. Very few people found the fortunes for which they were looking.

American Indians

In Twain's day, many white people feared American Indians. They were seen as hostile natives **impeding** the progress of America. As the population of white settlers grew, the need for land increased, which created conflict.

Various tribes viewed the land differently from white settlers. American Indians did not believe in owning land. Rather, they respected and shared the land they lived on. However, the U.S. government wanted to own the land officially. In 1830, Congress passed the Indian Removal Act. The act forced tribes to move to Indian Territory, the land west of the Mississippi River.

Reservation Life

Living on reservations was difficult. The American Indians were confined to specific areas and unable to hunt or farm. The government usually distributed their food. Their children had to go to reservation schools, often wearing American-style clothes and haircuts. It was nothing like the life they had known.

Later, as the country continued to expand westward, American Indians were pushed off that land as well. This time, the government forced tribes onto **reservations**. Some tribal members refused to relocate. They fought against the government's actions. Others attempted to **assimilate** into white culture. They hoped that by doing so they would avoid having to leave their homes.

The 1800s proved to be an agonizing time for American Indians. Many Indians died during the forced relocations. Others struggled to hold on to their cultures. Almost all American Indians faced **prejudice** and injustice.

An 1891 photograph was taken of the Miniconjou people near Pine Ridge Reservation in South Dakota.

Slavery

When Mark Twain was growing up, Missouri was a slave state. Slavery was a daily part of his life. There were approximately four million enslaved people in the South. Many enslaved workers were transported on the Mississippi River and were sold at auctions. In the Deep South, most slaves worked on plantations. In Hannibal, Missouri, some enslaved people worked in homes doing household chores. Owning slaves was seen by some people as an investment and a sign of wealth.

In the 1830s, people in the North banded together to try to end slavery. They were known as **abolitionists**. William Lloyd Garrison ran a newspaper that published articles about the evils of slavery. Frederick Douglass was an inspirational **orator**. He told powerful stories about his years spent in slavery. Harriet Beecher Stowe wrote the anti-slavery novel *Uncle Tom's Cabin*. Many other abolitionists worked endlessly and faced harsh criticisms and threats from others while trying to abolish slavery.

Ultimately, it would take the Civil War and an amendment to the U.S. Constitution to make slavery illegal. Yet even after the war, African Americans were denied equal rights. They continued to face harsh racism and prejudice in both the North and the South.

Twain's Views on Slavery

As a child, Twain was taught that there was nothing wrong with slavery. When his father could afford it, he owned and rented enslaved workers. It was not until Twain was an adult that he realized the evils of slavery and changed his views.

Uncle Dan'l

In the summers, Twain would visit his uncle's farm in the South. He spent a lot of time in the slave cabins, playing with the children and listening to the adults tell stories. Twain was especially fond of a man named Daniel Quarles, who he called Uncle Dan'l. The way Quarles told stories inspired Twain and shaped his storytelling techniques.

Time to Learn

By the mid-nineteenth century, many students across the United States attended public schools. However, when Twain began school around 1839, there weren't any public schools in his town. In Hannibal, there were two private schools for children, and Twain attended one of them. His parents paid twenty-five cents a week for him to go to the small schoolhouse made of logs.

Back then, most schools consisted of one room in which students from all grades sat and learned together with one teacher. The teacher was usually an unmarried woman. Schoolteachers were very strict. It was common for teachers to **lash** students who misbehaved. Boys and girls learned together. Reading, spelling, and mathematics were the subjects typically taught. Good manners and **piety** were also part of the curriculum. Textbooks were not invented yet, but Noah Webster (the same Webster who created the famous dictionary in 1828) made a spelling book that was widely used in schools. Teaching methods focused on memorization, recitation, and repetition.

School days were shorter and fewer in number than they are today. Students were needed at home to help with chores and family businesses, so they could not spend much time in school. Even so, while school was not **mandatory**, many families sent their children there.

Sunday School

In Twain's time, many children were sent to Sunday school each week. They studied the Bible and were taught moral principles.

After School

In the 1800s, most students finished school around the age of 14, or what is the equivalent to modern-day eighth grade. Attending college wasn't an option for a majority of students because parents needed their children to find jobs to help their families financially. They could not afford to have their children away at college instead of working.

When girls finished school, most of them continued the study of household duties at home. Boys were expected to find jobs outside the home or take up apprenticeships. They could learn how to make clothes or shoes or even study carpentry under master carpenters. Or they might become printers' apprentices like Twain did. There were several trades from which to choose.

Like so many other young men during that time, Twain did not attend college. Yet he was a very intelligent and learned man. A love for books, travel, and adventure served as Twain's education. Life experiences counted for a lot in those days and are what many people relied on to fill the gaps in their educations.

a woodworker sharing his tools and skills with an apprentice

THINK LINK

- How is school today different from school during Twain's time?
- Why do you think parents sent their children to school if it was not mandatory?
- How was being an apprentice similar to and different from being a student in school?

a tailor teaching a young boy his trade

Food of the Time

Twain often referenced food in his writing. In his travel book, *A Tramp Abroad*, Twain included a comprehensive list of all the American foods he wanted to eat once he returned home to the United States.

Most food was home cooked during Twain's time, and the ingredients were locally grown and purchased at public markets. Some families still farmed and hunted, and many kept vegetable gardens. People ate three meals a day starting with breakfast. Dinner began at one o'clock in the afternoon, usually the largest meal of the day. In the early evenings, people sat down to light suppers. Children were expected to practice good table manners at mealtimes.

The List

Twain's list of foods in *A Tramp Abroad* is quite long. It includes items such as American coffee, Southern-style fried chicken, San Francisco mussels, lake trout from Tahoe, Thanksgiving-style roast turkey, Boston bacon and beans, catsup, sweet milk, and apple pie.

One popular food was buckwheat pancakes. Buckwheat flour gives pancakes a nutty, earthy taste. Another favorite food was clabber, soured raw milk that was typically eaten like yogurt for breakfast. Common fruits included watermelon and fresh berries, along with pawpaws. Pawpaws resemble tropical fruits and taste like a mixture of mangos, bananas, and pineapples. Corn dodgers, small cakes made from fried cornmeal batter, were very popular, as was cornpone. This was a type of cornbread typically made without milk or eggs. Favorite meats were fried chicken, wild turkey, and roasted pig.

Huck's Meal

In *The Adventures of Huckleberry Finn*, Huck and Jim share many meals together during their journey. One of the meals Huck eats with Jim is "corn dodgers and buttermilk, and pork and cabbage, and greens."

All about Apparel

Twain once wrote, "Clothes make the man. Naked people have little or no influence on society." Humor aside, Twain was very interested in fashion, and clothing plays a crucial role in many of his works. *The Prince and the Pauper* is about two boys switching clothes and changing their lives as a result. In *A Connecticut Yankee in King Arthur's Court*, King Arthur dresses in peasant clothing and learns valuable life lessons.

In Twain's days, the clothing you wore was a reflection of your economic status. In the mid-1800s, wealthier people could afford finer materials and dressed more fashionably. They hired seamstresses or tailors to make their dresses and suits. For most people, clothes were still handmade using fabrics bought in town. Cotton was the most popular, affordable, and readily available fabric. Toward the end of the nineteenth century, more people were able to buy their clothes from local stores.

family photos taken during the 1890s

Sewing Machines

In 1851, Isaac Merritt Singer patented a new sewing machine. Although Singer wasn't the one to invent the sewing machine, he did create one that was easy to mass-produce and simple enough for the average person to use. This made making clothes at home much easier!

Boyhood Fashion

Boys in Twain's childhood hometown would have worn cotton shirts and heavy, durable trousers made of cotton or canvas that were held up by suspenders. In summertime, most boys ran barefoot and wore wide-brimmed straw hats to protect them from the hot sun. Only younger boys were allowed to wear short pants to help them stay cool, as it was considered inappropriate for teenage boys to do so. In the winter, boys wore wool vests, boots, and coats, if they could afford them. For fancier occasions, boys typically wore suits.

Fashion for Young Girls

Young girls wore dresses, which were mostly made of cotton or linen, year round. **Petticoats** were commonly worn under dresses to make them appear fuller. Bonnets that tied under the chin were worn to provide protection from the sun, while lace-up boots were common footwear. Girls were also expected to have their hair trimmed and tidy at all times. They were expected to keep their clothes neat and clean, too.

STOP! THINK...

Analyze the image above of Tom Sawyer's gang from a nineteenth century edition of *The Adventures of Huckleberry Finn*.

- ◎ What can you infer about the boys based on their clothing?

- ◎ In what ways are these boys dressed appropriately for their time?

- ◎ How does the boys' clothing in this illustration differ from clothing of children today?

Health and Home

As you can imagine, everyday family life in Twain's time was a little different from how it is today. There were no phones, cars, or electricity. Back then, men typically spent their days working on farms or at jobs in the cities. Women had their hands full inside the homes cooking, cleaning, and taking care of the children. Most families worked six days a week, and almost all families attended church on Sundays. Many people kept Sundays as strict days of rest.

In the Home

In Hannibal, Missouri, in the mid-1800s, families mainly lived in small homes, each consisting of one bedroom and a kitchen. Kitchens would have cast-iron stoves that were used for cooking and heating the homes. But there were no bathrooms! Back then, there were privies, or outhouses. Showers did not exist in the homes, and bathtubs were reserved for the wealthy. Thus, **basins** and pitchers of water were kept in the homes and were typically used for daily washings. At night, homes were lit using candles or **oil lamps**. Without electric lights, people generally went to sleep earlier than they do today and often rose with the sun.

No Toilet Paper Here!

Although toilet paper existed, people could not imagine spending their hard-earned money on something so frivolous. Instead, they used leaves, rags, cornhusks, or even more commonly, pages torn from catalogs or farmer's almanacs.

Where's the Bathroom?

Outhouses were enclosed structures made of wood or brick. They consisted of raised bench-like seats built over deep holes in the ground. They were generally set far from the houses to keep the smell away from the living quarters. When the holes got too full, they had to be emptied.

35

Violence and Crime

Twain took a lot of criticism about the violence and crimes in his books, which were often read by children. However, many of the children growing up in Hannibal at that time were no strangers to such offenses. Robberies and fights were commonplace. In fact, when Twain was a child, two murders occurred in his city. Once, he found the body of a runaway slave floating in the Mississippi River. A young Twain also witnessed a violent mob attacking an abolitionist.

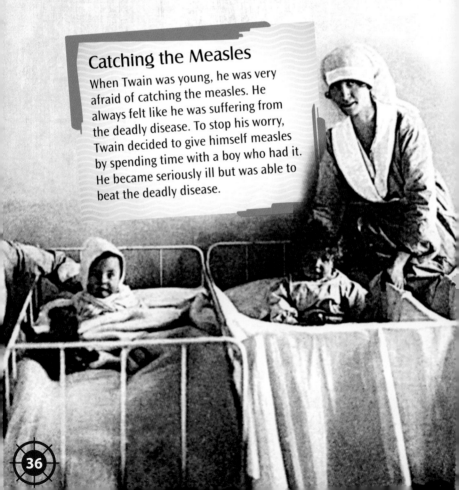

Catching the Measles

When Twain was young, he was very afraid of catching the measles. He always felt like he was suffering from the deadly disease. To stop his worry, Twain decided to give himself measles by spending time with a boy who had it. He became seriously ill but was able to beat the deadly disease.

Deadly Diseases

Violent crimes were not the only dangers facing children. There were also many diseases for which cures had not yet been found. Cities like Hannibal were prone to outbreaks of illnesses because of their proximity to the river. With so many people traveling the Mississippi River, germs were a constant threat.

Measles outbreaks took the lives of many children. Measles is a highly contagious disease that begins with a fever, a runny nose, and a sore throat. Later, a rash spreads over the body. Tuberculosis, or consumption, took many lives as well. This is a bacterial infection that attacks the lungs and is spread through coughing and sneezing. Today, we have **vaccines** to protect people against many diseases.

THINK LINK

◎ How are the dangers facing children today different from or similar to those that children faced in the past?

◎ Why do you think Twain included violence and crimes in his books that were read by children?

Frontier Games

While life could be tough and scary for children, it could also be exciting in ways children today may not experience. Children in the 1800s did not have video games or tablets, but they did have the outdoors to play sports and imaginative games. There weren't designated playgrounds, so children played wherever they found space.

Although Missouri had been a state since 1821, it still had a wildness to it that matched that of the wild western frontier. Thanks to Missouri's proximity to the Mississippi River, swimming was a popular pastime, as was fishing. Boys especially were known to hunt or pretend they were heroes from stories or history, such as Robin Hood. Twain and his friends pretended they were pirates looking for hidden treasures in caves around Hannibal.

Everyday items could be turned into toys. Sticks could be swords, and clothespins could be transformed into dolls. In addition to homemade toys, there were also toys that could be purchased in stores or from catalogs. Children often played with hoops, enjoyed rounds of hopscotch, or skipped rope.

Playful Pranks

One way kids entertained themselves was with pranks. When Twain was a boy, he loved playing pranks. One day, he told his mother he had gotten her a gift, and it was in his pocket. She reached in and pulled out a live bat!

Rolling in Wealth

In the famous whitewashing fence scene in *The Adventures of Tom Sawyer*, Tom tricks his friends into doing his work. They even pay Tom with toys and goods to work on the fence.

Let's Play!

Children relied heavily on their imaginations to entertain themselves in Twain's world, but they also had toys. Here are some of the toys that children could play with to fill their days.

Checkers—Challenge an opponent to this game of skill and strategy. The set comes with a two-color board and game pieces. Start thinking of clever moves now. You'll need them to beat your opponent!

Papier-mâché doll—This beautiful doll is imported from Germany. She stands about 14 inches (35.6 centimeters) high, with black hair and painted blue eyes and red lips. Her arms and legs are carved from wood. She wears a silk-and-lace-lined bodice and a skirt.

Dominoes—There are a number of challenging games you can play with this set of 28 wooden dominoes. Grab a friend, choose a game, and play to win!

Jacks—Remember, you can only use one hand with this challenging game. Can you toss the rubber ball and grab the jacks at the same time using the same hand? Give it a try!

Marbles—This game has been around for years, but your parents never had marbles like these. These new glass marbles make playing the old-style game fun again!

Spinning top—Hold the wooden peg between your thumb and forefinger, then snap your fingers together, and watch in amazement as the top spins and spins all by itself. This toy comes with instructions for thrilling games to play with your top!

Bandalore—What can you do with two metal disks and a string? Lots! Order this new take on an ancient Greek toy, and you'll get a list of bandalore tricks that will amaze your friends!

Jacob's Ladder—The blocks fall but never hit the floor. It's an optical illusion! Can you figure out how it works? This quiet toy is the only one approved for Sunday play.

American Adventures

Halley's Comet had ushered in one of America's most famous writers in 1835. Mark Twain passed away on April 21, 1910, the same year that Halley's comet returned to American skies. He left behind a **compilation** of witty works that tell the story of his life and times.

From running free on the banks of the Mississippi River to becoming a respected steamboat pilot and finally a beloved author, Twain's life experiences are immortalized in the pages of his stories. His world is reflected in his works. Stepping into Twain's world is like stepping back in time to a young country. The United States struggled with growing pains as did Twain. Serious historical conflicts were knit with riotous occasions of fun. America and Twain grew up together, influencing each other along the way.

Excerpt from Twain's Obituary

"Mark Twain's death has meant to Americans everywhere and in all walks of life what the death of no other American could have meant. His personality and his humor have been an integral part of American life for so long that it has seemed almost impossible to realize an America without him." —*The New York Times*

Glossary

abolitionists—people who wanted to end slavery

assimilate—to cause a person or group to become part of a larger different society or culture

basins—large bowls or containers used to hold liquids

comet—an object in outer space made of ice and dust that develops a visible tail of gas as it passes near the sun

compilation—a collection of works, such as writing

epithets—offensive words used to describe a person or group of people

frontiers—undeveloped areas or regions on the edge of a settled part of a country

impeding—interfering or slowing progress or movement

impish—mischievous; having a playful desire to cause trouble

keelboats—long, slim boats with sails and pieces of wood at the bottom to provide stability

lash—to strike a person with something such as a whip or a stick

mandatory—required by law or rules

migrants—people who move from one place to another to find work

oil lamps—lamps that burn oil such as kerosene to produce light

orator—a skillful and powerful public speaker

outlandish—bizarre or strange; extremely different from what is considered normal

perks—bonuses or extras received for doing a good job

petticoats—full and often ruffled skirts worn under dresses

piety—deeply religious devotion to God

plantations—large areas of land where crops (such as cotton) are grown

prejudice—an unfair dislike for a person or group based on race, gender, or religion

premature—born too early; born before 37 weeks of pregnancy

reservations—areas of land in the United States where American Indians were mandated to live

secede—to formally withdraw from a state, nation, or organization

Union—a group of states ruled by one government

vaccines—microbes that are injected into a person to help create immunity to a disease

Index

Check It Out!

This is an abbreviated list of Mark Twain's books with their original publication dates.

Adventures of Huckleberry Finn, The (1884)
Adventures of Tom Sawyer, The (1876)
Connecticut Yankee in King Arthur's Court, A (1889)
Innocents Abroad, The (1869)
Life on the Mississippi (1883)
Prince and the Pauper, The (1881)
Roughing It (1872)

Books

Aller, Susan Bivin. 2006. *Mark Twain.* Lerner Publications Company.

Fleischman, Sid. 2008. *The Trouble Begins at 8: A Life of Mark Twain in the Wild, Wild West.* Greenwillow Books.

Katz, Harry L., and The Library of Congress. 2014. *Mark Twain's America: A Celebration in Words and Images.* Little Brown and Company.

Lasky, Kathryn. 1998. *A Brilliant Streak: The Making of Mark Twain.* Harcourt Brace & Company.

Twain, Mark. 2010. *Autobiography of Mark Twain: The Complete and Authoritative Edition Volumes 1–3.* University of California Press.

Websites

PBS. *Mark Twain: Known to Everyone, Liked by All.* http://www.pbs.org/marktwain/index.html.

The Mark Twain House and Museum. http://www.marktwainhouse.org/about/about_us.php.

University of Virginia Library. *Mark Twain in His Times.* http://twain.lib.virginia.edu/index2.html.

Try It!

Mark Twain was known for taking everyday observations and using humor to explain them. Imagine that, like Twain, you are sent out of your country on business but will have time to be a tourist as well. Choose a destination that you've always wanted to visit. Observe the environment and the people.

- Where do you want to go? Be specific. Choose something from that culture: food, a piece of art, architecture, music, or another form of entertainment.

- Brainstorm as many adjectives and adverbs about your selection as you can.

- Create a postcard of the chosen place. On one side, draw a picture, and on the other side, write a note to someone back home.

- In the note, use humor, the way Twain did to describe your visit and the part of that culture you chose to detail further.

About the Author

Torrey Maloof loves researching and writing books about history's most interesting people and events. She didn't grow up on the banks of the Mississippi River like Twain did, but rather on the sandy shores of Southern California. She often can be found reading in the sun on local beaches. Torrey also loves chasing after her young niece, Cordelia, who, like her aunt, loves books and the beach. The two also hold a special place in their hearts for Disneyland and frequently visit the magical theme park together.